COOL CASTLES AND PALACES
GRAND PALACE

by Clara Bennington

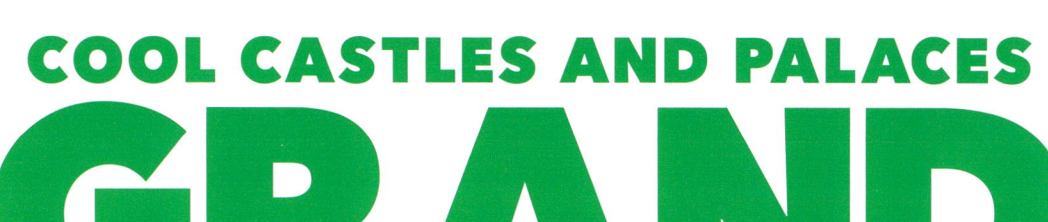

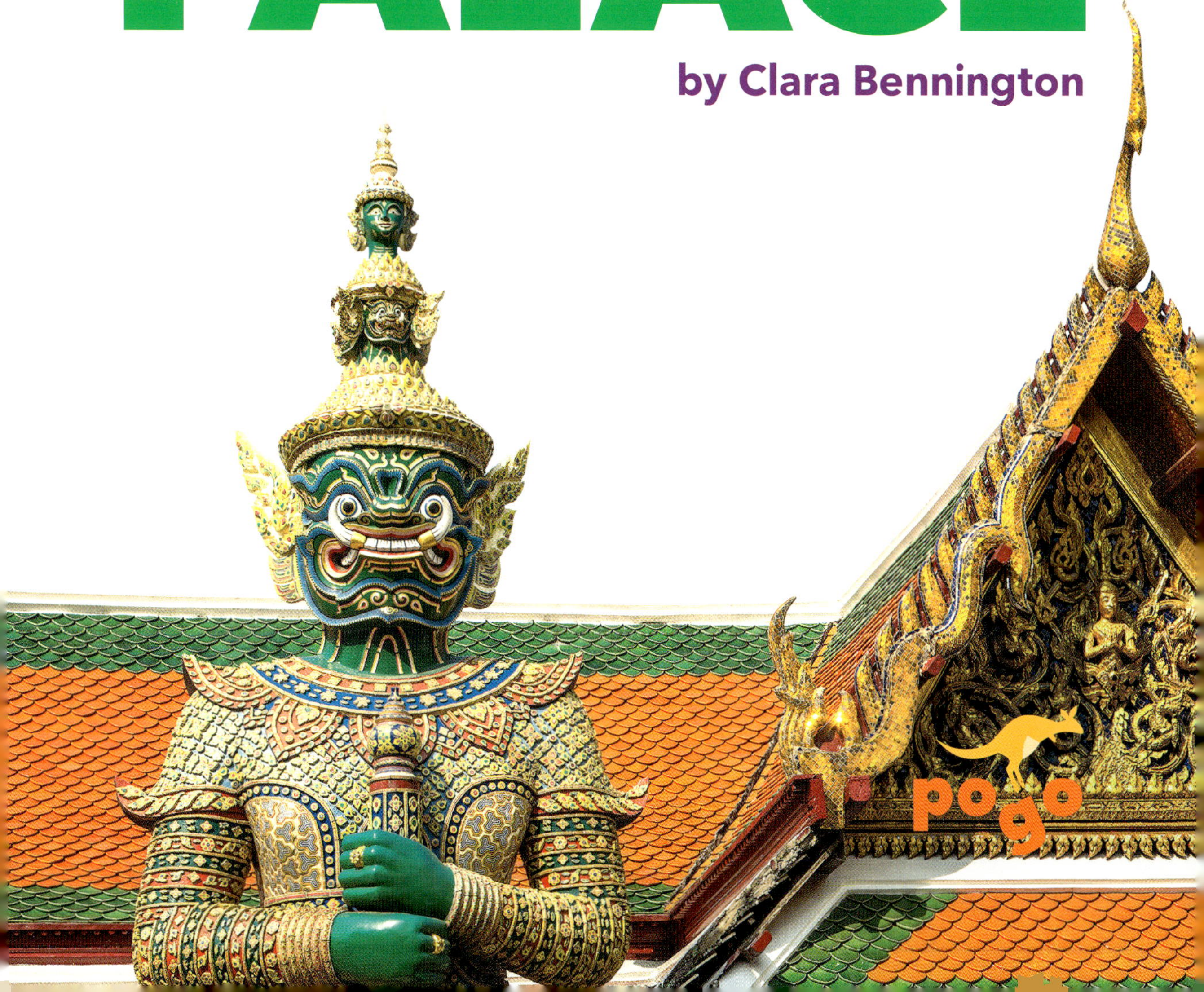

Ideas for Parents and Teachers

Pogo Books let children practice reading informational text while introducing them to nonfiction features such as headings, labels, sidebars, maps, and diagrams, as well as a table of contents, glossary, and index.

Carefully leveled text with a strong photo match offers early fluent readers the support they need to succeed.

Before Reading

- "Walk" through the book and point out the various nonfiction features. Ask the student what purpose each feature serves.
- Look at the glossary together. Read and discuss the words.

Read the Book

- Have the child read the book independently.
- Invite him or her to list questions that arise from reading.

After Reading

- Discuss the child's questions. Talk about how he or she might find answers to those questions.
- Prompt the child to think more. Ask: Did you know about the Grand Palace before you read this book? What more would you like to learn?

Pogo Books are published by Jump!
5357 Penn Avenue South
Minneapolis, MN 55419
www.jumplibrary.com

Copyright © 2020 Jump!
International copyright reserved in all countries.
No part of this book may be reproduced in any form without written permission from the publisher.

Library of Congress Cataloging-in-Publication Data

Names: Bennington, Clara, author.
Title: Grand Palace / by Clara Bennington.
Description: Minneapolis, MN: Jump!, Inc., 2020.
Series: Cool castles and palaces
Includes index. | Audience: Age 7-10.
Identifiers: LCCN 2018061513 (print)
LCCN 2019002847 (ebook)
ISBN 9781641288682 (ebook)
ISBN 9781641288675 (hardcover : alk. paper)
Subjects: LCSH: Phraráatchawang éChan (Phitsanulok, Thailand) —Juvenile literature. Nobility—Thailand—Juvenile literature.
Classification: LCC DS588.P45 (ebook)
LCC DS588.P45 B46 2020 (print)
DDC 305.5/2209593—dc23
LC record available at https://lccn.loc.gov/2018061513

Editor: Jenna Trnka
Designer: Molly Ballanger

Photo Credits: Armpsth/Shutterstock, cover; S-F/Shutterstock, 1; Irainy/Shutterstock, 3; SOUTHERNTraveler/Shutterstock, 4; bangongseal324/iStock, 5; Stock Connection/SuperStock, 6-7; apiguide/Shutterstock, 8-9; Nuamfolio/Shutterstock, 10; southtownboy/iStock, 11; Golf_chalermchai/Shutterstock, 12-13; anek.soowannaphoom/Shutterstock, 14-15; kerochan/Shutterstock, 16; WichitS/Getty, 17; cowardlion/Shutterstock, 18-19; robertharding/Alamy, 20-21; Merydolla/Shutterstock, 23.

Printed in the United States of America at Corporate Graphics in North Mankato, Minnesota.

TABLE OF CONTENTS

CHAPTER 1
Statues and Spires 4

CHAPTER 2
The Emerald Buddha 10

CHAPTER 3
At the Palace 16

QUICK FACTS & TOOLS
At a Glance 22
Glossary 23
Index 24
To Learn More 24

CHAPTER 1
STATUES AND SPIRES

Welcome to the Grand Palace! It is in Bangkok, Thailand. It was built in 1782. This is when Bangkok became the **capital**.

Statues decorate the palace **complex**. These look like they are holding up a building!

CHAPTER 1

Grand Residence

CHAPTER 1

More than 100 buildings make up the complex. The Grand Residence has seven buildings. They are all connected. This is where kings once lived.

The Grand Palace Hall was built in 1877. British **architects** designed it. It was the first building in Thailand to have electricity! It is now used for formal meals.

WHAT DO YOU THINK?

Many buildings here have spires. What if you could design a palace? How many rooms would it have? How would you decorate it? Why?

CHAPTER 1

CHAPTER 2
THE EMERALD BUDDHA

Buddhism is a big part of the **culture** here. A special **chapel** was built. It is the Chapel of the Emerald Buddha.

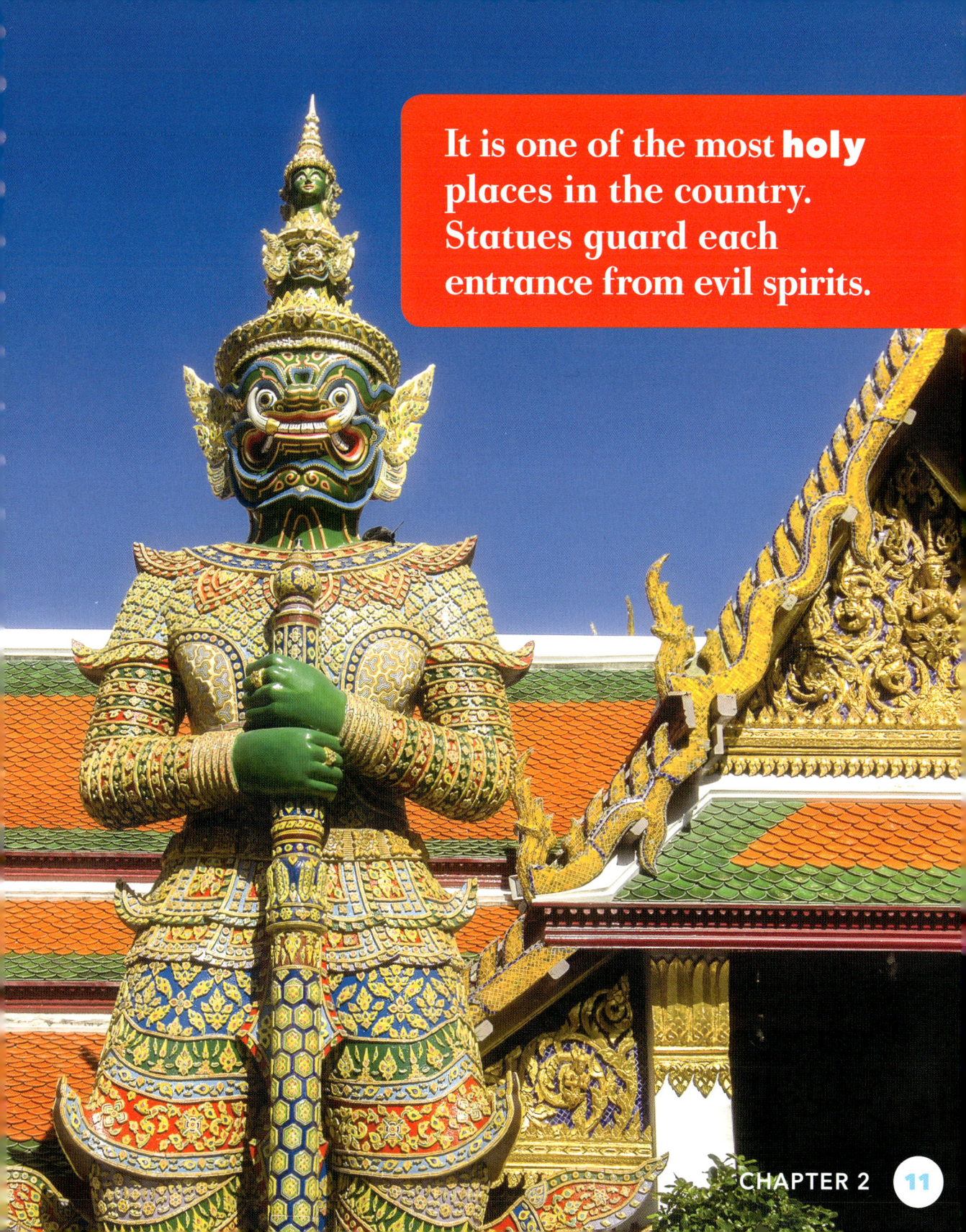

It is one of the most **holy** places in the country. Statues guard each entrance from evil spirits.

CHAPTER 2

The Emerald Buddha is small. It is only two feet (66 centimeters) high! But it is very holy. It sits on a golden **shrine**.

DID YOU KNOW?

The buddha is made of **jade**. It has three different robes. A member of the **royal** family changes them. There is one for each season.

CHAPTER 2

The Emerald Buddha was going to be in the Royal Pantheon. It was built in 1856. But the building was too small for **ceremonies**. It is now used to honor past kings. Statues of them are here.

Royal Pantheon

TAKE A LOOK!

The Royal Pantheon is part of Wat Phra Kaew. Many buildings make up this **temple**. See some of their uses!

CHAPEL OF THE EMERALD BUDDHA
houses the Emerald Buddha

ROYAL PANTHEON
has statues of past kings

PHRA MONDOP
library that has many texts about Buddha

GOLDEN STUPA
houses remains of Buddha

CHAPTER 2　15

CHAPTER 3
AT THE PALACE

Three spires are near the front. These are the tallest parts of the complex. The Golden Stupa is one.

Golden Stupa

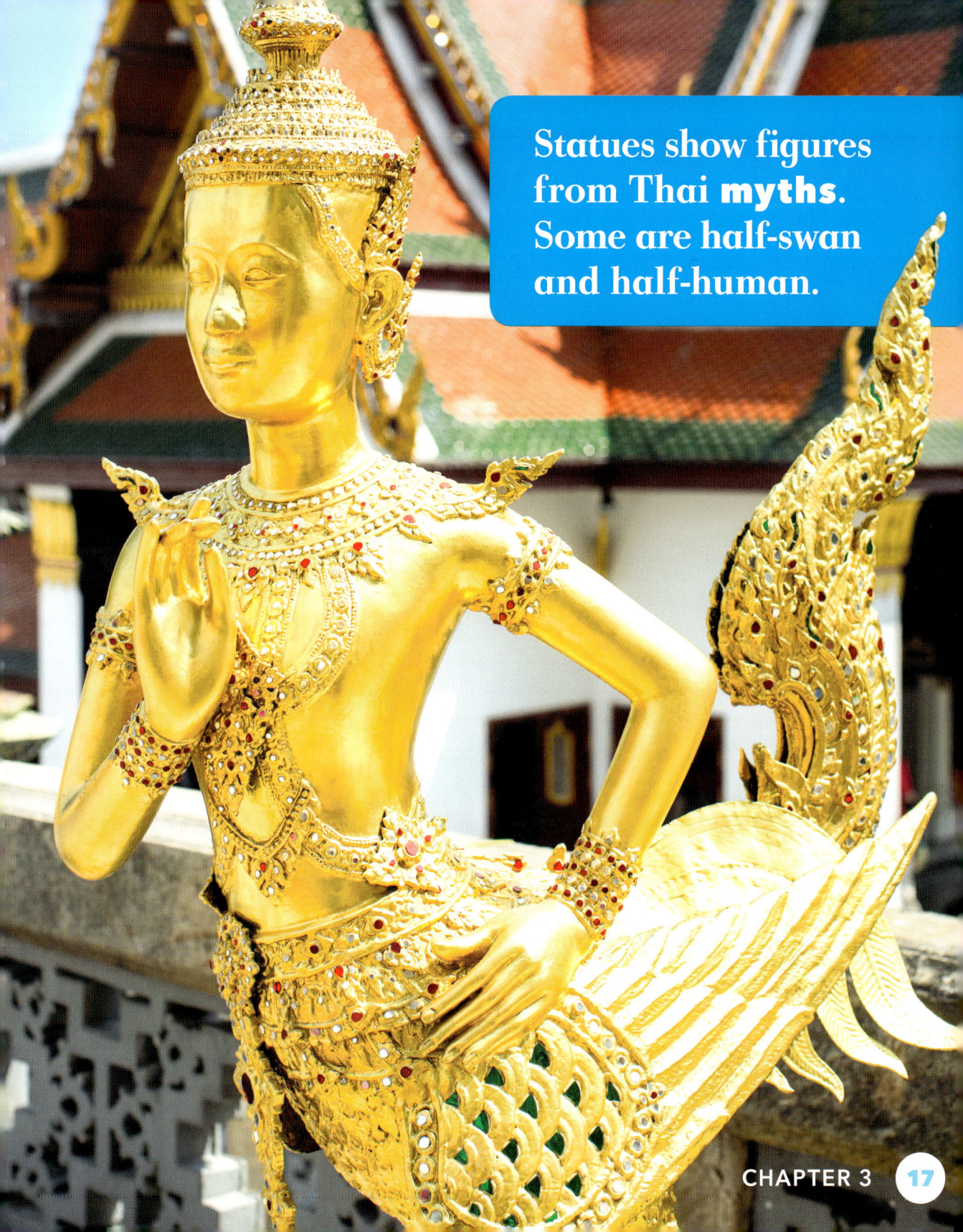

Statues show figures from Thai **myths**. Some are half-swan and half-human.

CHAPTER 3 17

Coronations and other events still take place here. This is the Grand Spired Hall. Funerals take place here.

CHAPTER 3

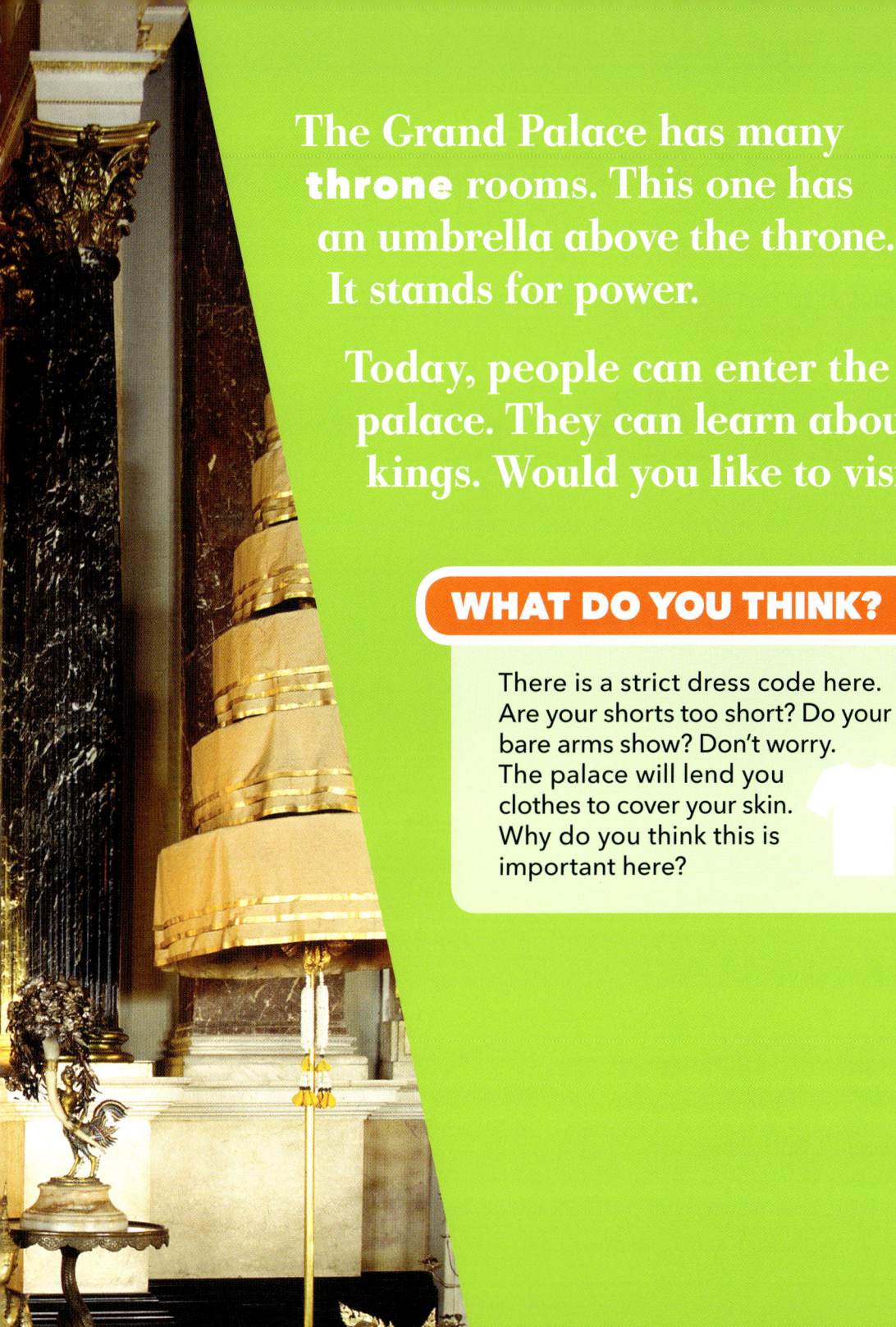

The Grand Palace has many **throne** rooms. This one has an umbrella above the throne. It stands for power.

Today, people can enter the palace. They can learn about kings. Would you like to visit?

WHAT DO YOU THINK?

There is a strict dress code here. Are your shorts too short? Do your bare arms show? Don't worry. The palace will lend you clothes to cover your skin. Why do you think this is important here?

QUICK FACTS & TOOLS

AT A GLANCE

GRAND PALACE

Location: Bangkok, Thailand
Year Construction Began: 1782
Size: 60 acres (24.3 hectares)
Number of Buildings: More than 100

Current Use: Museum and occasional government events
Average Number of Visitors Each Year: 8 million

GLOSSARY

architects: People who design buildings and oversee how they are built.

Buddhism: A way of life based on the teachings of Buddha, a man who lived in India around 500 BCE.

capital: A city where government leaders meet.

ceremonies: Formal events that mark important occasions.

chapel: A small church.

complex: A group of buildings that are near each other and are used for similar purposes.

coronations: Ceremonies in which kings, queens, or other rulers are crowned.

culture: The ideas, customs, traditions, and ways of life of a group of people.

holy: Related to or belonging to a god or higher being.

jade: A hard, blue-green stone used for making ornaments or jewelry.

myths: Old stories that express the beliefs or history of a group of people or explain natural events.

royal: Related to a king or queen or a member of his or her family.

shrine: A building or structure that contains objects associated with a holy person.

temple: A building used for worship.

throne: A special chair for a ruler to sit on during a ceremony.

QUICK FACTS & TOOLS 23

INDEX

architects 8
Bangkok, Thailand 4
Buddha 15
Buddhism 10
ceremonies 14
Chapel of the Emerald Buddha 10, 15
dress code 21
Emerald Buddha 13, 14, 15
Golden Stupa 15, 16
Grand Palace Hall 8
Grand Residence 7
Grand Spired Hall 18
kings 7, 14, 15, 18, 21
myths 17
royal family 13
Royal Pantheon 14, 15
shrine 13
spires 8, 16
statues 5, 11, 14 ,15, 17
Thailand 4, 8
throne rooms 21
Wat Phra Kaew 15

TO LEARN MORE

Finding more information is as easy as 1, 2, 3.

❶ Go to www.factsurfer.com
❷ Enter "GrandPalace" into the search box.
❸ Choose your book to see a list of websites.

QUICK FACTS & TOOLS